EAST GRINSTEAD - THEN & NOW

Ron Michell and David Gould

Other Sussex books from Middleton Press, available from local booksellers:

Midhurst Town – Then & Now
An album illustrating how little this charming country town has been affected by the passage of time.

The Green Roof of Sussex
A refreshing summer amble along the 80 miles of the South Downs Way.

Branch Lines to Midhurst
Branch Lines to Horsham
Branch Line to Selsey
Branch Lines to East Grinstead

South Coast Railways –
Brighton to Eastbourne
Brighton to Worthing
Worthing to Chichester
Chichester to Portsmouth

First published 1985

ISBN 0 906520 17 7

Phototypeset by CitySet Ltd · Chichester 573270

Cover design – Deborah Goodridge

Published by Middleton Press
Easebourne Lane
Midhurst, West Sussex.
GU29 9AZ

Printed & bound by Biddles Ltd.,
Guildford and Kings Lynn.

CONTENTS

INTRODUCTION

An iceberg, they say, shows only one sixth of its bulk above the surface; the same might be true of the contents of this book. There may have been towns more often photographed than East Grinstead, but few can equal the number of pictures taken through the years of the half mile between Sackville College and Railway Approach. From the 1860s until the present day talented photographers have recorded every change and every mood. Our task, therefore, has not been to search frantically for material, but rather to reject with some mental anguish dozens of pictures that fully deserved a place in this book. Our choice has, in a sense, been made more difficult by the help given by several of our friends. Nick Stephanakis has generously made available for our use the contents of his vast collection of photographic prints and so have the Trustees of the East Grinstead Town Museum. M.J. Leppard, the Hon Curator, has also helped in a different way by his careful reading of the text. His comments have helped both the content and the accuracy of our work, though it must be said that any mistakes that remain are in no way attributable to his guidance. They are all our own.

The last comprehensive history of East Grinstead was written by Wallace H. Hills and published in 1906 and his book is a rare treasure for those who are fortunate enough to possess a copy. We know, through our work with the Town Museum, that there are constant requests for a new history of the town. We do not pretend, or even wish, that the present volume will do more than titillate without satisfying that demand. We earnestly hope that a full and scholarly history of East Grinstead will eventually be forthcoming.

Meanwhile we offer our thanks to all the other people who have helped in the production of this offering. David Kirk has allowed us to use several of his unique prints. Thanks are also due to Malcolm Powell for permission to reproduce two views by Harold Connold, and to Norman Sherry for the delightfully nostalgic final illustration. Finally our gratitude goes to Vic Mitchell of Middleton Press for his advice and willingness to undertake production of this venture.

HISTORICAL BACKGROUND

East Grinstead was founded during the early 13th century by Gilbert d'Aquila, Lord of Pevensey. The great wealden forest, of which Ashdown is only a remnant, had once been a barrier that separated Sussex from Surrey; but by the 1200s increasing settlement made a market, and perhaps a centre of administration, necessary amongst the farms and hamlets that had been cleared in the district. The town was also to be a convenient staging point along the track that led from London to Lewes, and its hill-top church became a landmark for many miles around.

The pattern of the medieval town planner is still evident. The broad High Street, designed as a market place, was lined on either side by long narrow plots called 'portlands'. On these strips, each 10 metres (32 feet) wide, the burgesses of the new town built their homes in the fashion of the times, with halls open to the rafters above and a small upper chamber at one end called a solar. Cooking was done at the open hearth or in a separate kitchen behind. No less than 19 buildings of this type, though much altered through the years, survive from the 14th and 15th centuries while another 13 were built during the Tudor and Stuart periods.

The town, at the height of its prosperity during the 17th century, remained small with little more than three hundred inhabitants including traders, shopkeepers and small manufacturers as well as agricultural workers. It was however an important centre, not only because of its annual fairs and weekly markets, but also for the flourishing wealden iron industry and as it was one of the places where the assizes were held. Thereafter there was a slow decline in prosperity; in 1822 William Cobbett called it a "rotten borough, a very shabby place". The "rotten borough" referred to the fact that from 1301 the town had returned two members to Parliament – a privilege that was taken away in the reforms of 1832. The "shabbiness", for us, had the advantage that few owners wished, or could afford, to rebuild the old timber houses whose massive oak frameworks, chopped about, altered and adapted, still remained capable of supporting the heavy roofs of stone slabs which had been transported from the Horsham area during the middle ages.

Prosperity returned slowly after the building of the town's first railway line in 1855, and, as the period of revival coincides with the work of William Harding, the first local photographer, we possess a nearly complete record of the town's appearance during the last hundred-odd years.

PHOTOGRAPHERS OF THE PAST

Historians owe a great deal to photographers and their work, and those of East Grinstead are no exception. The local professional photographers in the 1902-14 period issued much of their work as postcards, being sold either from their studios or at stationers in the town. As the local newspapers carried no pictures, big events were photographed by these professionals, the results being assured of a good sale.

Little is known as yet of East Grinstead's professional photographers, but below are some notes on those whose work is represented in this book.

HAROLD CONNOLD

Assisted Ernest Watts, photographer, 1907-08; took over the business in 1926 and ran it from 23 High Street (later 15 High

Street) until his retirement in 1959. His output was prodigious, both in outdoor work and studio portraiture. He photographed most of the successive chairmen of the urban district council, becoming one himself in 1949-50. Many views of East Grinstead are his work, and he went into the surrounding villages too. He produced a range of postcards (about 200) based on some of his photographs, although this represented only a tiny proportion of his work. Some of his negatives remain in the care of Mr Malcolm Powell, the present photographer at 15 High Street.

WILLIAM and ARTHUR HARDING

William Harding, native of East Grinstead, was in business in Middle Row as a photographer in the 1860s. His best-known work is the range of postcards, later printings of his early work, depicting scenes of the town in the 1860s, always lettered "ET. GRINSTEAD" with a date (not always a correct date). He became manager of the new Elephant's Head coffee tavern and, after the failure of that enterprise, was librarian of the Literary and Scientific Institute from 1887 almost until his death at the age of 84 on 12 May 1922.

Arthur Harding, his only son, inherited William's photographic abilities and it is probable that the enormous series of postcards issued in the early 1900s was his work; they are identified by a rubber-stamped "Harding, Photo., East Grinstead" on the back. It is known that he photographed the unveiling of the war memorial on 27 July 1922.

V.E. MORRIS

Son of the postmaster at 65 Lingfield Road, Victor Emanuel Morris succeeded to the grocery business and ran it with his sisters Mary and Joanna until well into the 1930s. So far as can be judged he was an amateur photographer, with a darkroom at the back of the shop, but issued several postcards of local views, on sale at his shop. He was a Wesleyan, and a conscientious objector during the Great War. In April 1923 he won first prize in the open class for lantern slides at a photographic exhibition in Lewes and in January 1935 he lectured on "More Sussex pictures" at a Moat Fellowship meeting.

WILLIAM PAGE

Operating from Moat Studio, 5 Moat Road, from c. 1884 to c. 1914, he acquired the business, premises and apparently the stock of H.T. and M.A. Melville, who were there in the 1870s. William Page's work appeared in a town guide of 1909 and in several subsequent guides. He also issued several picture postcards of street scenes; many are faintly impressed in one corner "Wm Page, Moat Studio, East Grinstead". He was a superb photographer, most of his views being of high artistic merit.

ERNEST WATTS

His studio was at 23 High Street and he was in business until 1926, when Harold Connold took it over. He specialised in portraiture; outdoor work was seldom done. In January 1913 he had five photographs accepted and hung at the Northern Photographic Society's exhibition held at Manchester Art Gallery. Most of the prominent people in East Grinstead were photographed by Watts at some period.

EDGAR KINSEY

This pnotographer traded rather grandly as the East Grinstead Photo Company, although his studio, at 24 Railway Approach, was quite a small one. He undertook both portraiture, street photography and the recording of big "events" and ceremonies. He was also a picture-frame maker, this work being done for a time at 5 Middle Row. His street photographs are of interest in that he covered several roads neglected by other photographers, and they were issued as postcards, at least one being printed in reverse – a surprising slip for a professional. He was in business between about 1909 and 1930.

The Town Map of 1841, prepared for the Tithe Commissioners, shows the limits of the ancient borough and how little it had grown since its foundation; practically all the building was still limited to both sides of the High Street. Those on the south side, and many of those on the north, can be identified by a survey that was made in 1564 and most are standing today. The Portlands show up clearly, though even by Elizabethan times a number of the wealthier owners had been able to combine two or three plots, giving space for more imposing dwellings, and making the enclosures more practicable. To the north, beyond the limits of the map, the London Road passed, unenclosed, across the town common that sloped down towards the Surrey border and the hamlet of Felbridge.

The Ordnance Survey map of 1899 shows that the town doubled its size since the previous map was produced. It had become the centre of a railway system that radiated in all directions. The gaps along the London Road were fully built-up, mostly with shops that competed with those in the High Street. Terraces lined the older roads of the town while a whole new area of mainly villa development had grown around the railway cuttings in the north. It was still, however, a small country town whose fairs, markets and shops catered for the needs of the agricultural district around. Growth of the town was, to some extent, inhibited by large private parks, East Court, Imberhorne and Placelands, around its borders and by 1900 the first phase of growth was complete. The second phase of expansion would not take place for another sixty years.

The 1931 map shows the town centre fully built up except for the Place Land estate. Road names have assumed their modern form. Glen Vue Road has become Railway Approach, the ill-named Cemetery Road is now Queens Road. King Street opposite has yet to be built. At a scale of 25" to the mile all public buildings are marked which will assist readers less familiar with the town to locate the photographs that follow. The map does not cover all the roads illustrated in this book, but those who wish for further detail

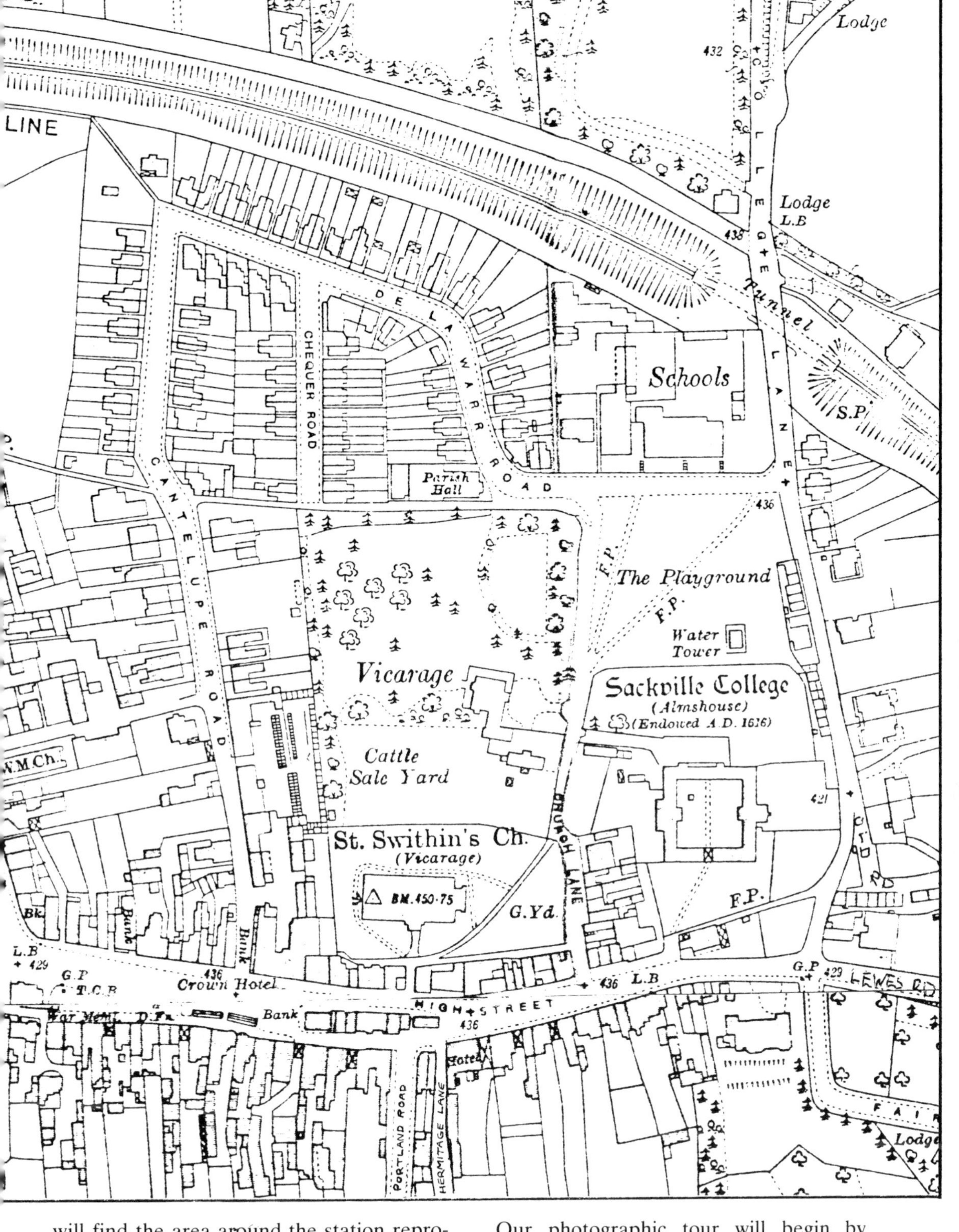

will find the area around the station reproduced to the same scale in the companion volume to this, "Branch Lines to East Grinstead".

Our photographic tour will begin by exploring the area of the old town, passing along the south side of the High Street to its junction with the London Road and returning on the opposite side towards the parish church.

BLACKWELL HOLLOW

1. The town stands upon an outcrop of sandstone 138 metres (450 ft) above sea level at its highest point. From all directions, except the north-west, the approach is steep, and old tracks, worn down by weather, wheels and the feet of its inhabitants became deep 'hollow ways'. The passing years have made little change to this 1907 view.
(F. Frith & Co.)

2. Until the early 19th century the eastern approach also passed through a steep sandstone cutting as this painting by J.L. Bourne (c.1820) shows. In 1826 a new road was laid out that bypassed and partly filled in the cutting in order to give a gentler gradient.
(J.L. Bourne)

3. The old road winds its way from the present round-about to Sackville College. This modern view looks in the opposite direction and is taken from a point that roughly coincides with the high bank seen just below the church tower in the Bourne painting.
(R. Michell)

THE OLD ROAD

THE TOLL GATE

4. The roads of Sussex were notorious; rutted, unmetalled, and usually impassable during the winter months. Some improvement was made in 1718 when the first local turnpike act was passed. The East Grinstead gate stood at the Forest Row exit of the town until soon after this picture was taken in 1865. The small stone cottage from which the 'pikeman' collected his dues can be seen on the left, today only its name remains, but just beyond was the town 'lock-up' and a careful observer will find the small cell window in the surviving building. (W. Harding)

From *Britannia Depicta* 1731

East-Grinstead
SUSSEX
Turnpike.
Wednesday
17 April 1754
One Shilling.

SOUTHDOWN AND EAST GRINSTEAD BREWERIES,
LIMITED,
Brewers, Maltsters, Wine, Spirit, Bottled Ale and Stout Merchants,
THE BREWERY, EAST GRINSTEAD,
AND AT LEWES AND CUCKFIELD.

P.A.	LIGHT DINNER ALE ... 1/- per Gal.		XXX.	STRONG ALE	1/4 per Gal.
I.P.A.	INDIA PALE ALE... 1/4 to 1/6	„	XXXX.	EXTRA STRONG ALE...	2/- „
X.	MILD BROWN ALE ... 10d.	„		PORTER	1/- „
XX.	MILD BROWN ALE ... 1/-	„		STOUT...	1/4 „
				DOUBLE STOUT	1/6 „

Supplied in 4½ 6, 9, 18 and 36 Gallon Casks.

Sole Local Agents for the Famous GODES-BERGER WATER
AND FOR
TEACHER'S HIGHLAND CREAM WHISKEY.

ORDERS addressed THE MANAGER, THE BREWERY, EAST GRINSTEAD, have prompt attention.
Telephone No. 22.

SACKVILLE COLLEGE

5. A tour of the town should properly begin with its largest and most important historic building. Founded in 1609 by the will of Robert Sackville the second Earl of Dorset, it was not completed for another ten years through negligence on the part of his successor. It is not a college as most people today would understand it; the word has an older meaning of a community of people. It is, in fact, an almshouse. The College has changed little since 1900 when this view was taken, although the corner of College Lane has. (William Page)

6. The Sackville family were already large landowners in the town and they continued to exert an influence, particularly over the election of the members of parliament. They also retained a suite of rooms in the college, a useful lodging after a day spent hunting in Ashdown Forest, or when business, such as the Assizes, made a town residence necessary. (N. Stephanakis)

7. John Mason Neale was the most distinguished of the College Wardens. Historian, linguist, and the writer of many well-known hymns, his period of office from 1846 to 1866 was not without disturbances. His most notable act was the foundation in 1855 of the Society of St Margaret, a sisterhood of nuns formed to nurse the sick poor in the isolated cottages of Ashdown Forest and the surrounding country. To the general public he will be best known as the author of the carol 'Good King Wenceslas'. (D. Kirk collection)

THE HIGH STREET

8. This earliest view of the High Street dates from about 1864. Few towns can show so little change; after 120 years every building, except for the *Rose and Crown* rebuilt in 1939, retains its outline today. The large block on the right of the picture was used by the St Margaret's Sisterhood until the convent at the other end of the town was built. (W. Harding)

9. Cyclists and tourists will look in vain for the Olde Easte Greenstede Cafe. It is now a private dwelling. But in other respects this 1903 view has changed little. Cromwell House (the name is a fantasy) still dominates this part of the street as it did when it was new in 1599. The influential Payne family, ironmasters of the town, lived here. Then it was 'The Great House'. (W. Harding)

10. One could not guess that Cromwell House was devastated by fire in 1928. It was carefully restored by Walter Godfrey. (R. Michell)

Ye Olde Caste Greenstede Cafe
FOR
CYCLISTS MOTORISTS
& TOURISTS
E. GRINSTEAD

11. Beyond Cromwell House is Sackville House, built during the early Tudor period. The only change since the earliest photographs were taken is that the plaster that once hid its timber framework has been removed. It retains today much of its portland and through a small spyhole in its gate may be glimpsed one of the most glorious views in Sussex. Next to it (on the right) Amherst House is one of the three oldest houses in East Grinstead; it was built within a century of the town's foundation. (R. Michell)

→

12. The fine brickwork, distinctive small-paned windows and heavy cornice would make it certain that Dorset House was built during the reign of Queen Anne even if the date were not recorded on the rainwater head. It is 1705, but the house contains Tudor panelling obviously re-used from an earlier building. (R. Michell)

WILLIAM PAGE,

PHOTOGRAPHER,

. . MOAT STUDIO . .

5, Moat Road,
EAST GRINSTEAD.

SPECIALITY **PORTRAITS in the STUDIO.**

— ALL DESCRIPTIONS OF OUTDOOR PHOTOGRAPHY.—

Carbon, Platinotype & Bromide ENLARGEMENTS.

MINIATURE PHOTOGRAPHS, PLAIN OR COLOURED.

Amateurs' work Developed, Retouched and Printed.

POST CARDS.

The *Dorset Arms* was the principal coaching inn of the town. It has had several names and became *Dorset Arms* only in 1790 after the closure of *Dorset Head* on the other side of the High Street. It was the *Ounce and Ivy Bush* in 1605, the *Cat* as early as 1636, while the *Newe Inn* antedates them all.

Travellers to Brighton via Lewes halted here in the early days of coaching. It was no coincidence that the Batchelar family owned both the coach and inn. There was some indignation when a rival, J. Tubb, announced that his 'Flying Machine' would do the journey in one day. Batchelar reduced his fares and in the *Lewes Journal* for November 1762 Tubb replied:

THIS IS TO INFORM THE PUBLIC that, on Monday, the 1st of November instant, the LEWES and BRIGHTHELMSTON FLYING MACHINE began going in *one day*, and continues twice a week during the Winter Season to Lewes only; sets out from the White Hart, at Lewes, MONDAYS and THURSDAYS at Six o'clock in the Morning, and returns from the Golden Cross, at Charing Cross, TUESDAYS and SATURDAYS, at the same hour.

Performed by J. TUBB.

N.B.—Gentlemen, Ladies, and others, are desired to look narrowly into the Meanness and Design of the other Flying Machine to Lewes and Brighthelmston, in lowering his prices, whether 'tis thro' conscience or an endeavour to suppress me. If the former is the case, think how you have been used for a great number of years, when he engrossed the whole to himself, and kept you two days upon the road, going fifty miles. If the latter, and he should be lucky enough to succeed in it, judge whether he wont return to his old prices, when you cannot help yourselves, and use you as formerly. As I have, then, been the remover of this obstacle, which you have all granted by your great encouragement to me hitherto, I, therefore, hope for the continuance of your favours, which will entirely frustrate the deep-laid schemes of my great opponent, and lay a lasting obligation on,—Your very humble Servant,

J. TUBB.

13. & 14. Astonishing continuity! Only the veteran car parked outside the *Dorset Arms* shows that eighty years separate the two pictures. (F. Frith & Co. and R. Michell)

16. H.H. Nutt's fleet of cabs c.1906. No such splendid sight will greet the traveller in Portland Road today; there will only be a depressing row of parked cars. The many differing styles of brickwork on the wall behind the cabs are testimony to the centuries of change that have taken place. The jumble of roofs behind belongs to Wilmington, one of the oldest and most complex of the town's houses. (E. Watts)

15. The modern walker will pass behind Middle Row, crossing the entrance to Hermitage Lane (another ancient hollow way) and of Portland Road. These ancient cottages were demolished when Portland Road was laid out in 1891. (W. Page)

17. The total absence of cars is not solely due to snow – it was also Christmas Day in 1981! (D. Gould)

18. From the narrow roadway Wilmington House makes one of the most attractive views in the town. The passageway in the centre of the picture is almost all that remains of a hall house built about 1350. Once it was a part of the original hall, but the house was extended by the section nearer to the camera some 200 years later. On the extreme left the brickwork is part of a further addition built during the 18th century. (R. Michell)

19. All these cottages were standing when Elizabeth I was on the throne; only the shop fronts and the proprietors' names have changed since 1903. Wilmington is on the left of the picture. Notice the roofs of Horsham slabs – typical of all our oldest buildings. (F. Frith & Co.)

20. As one emerges from behind Middle Row the full width of the town marketplace can be appreciated. The picture, dating from the early 1900s, is peaceful but the space was sometimes the centre for stirring events. During the reign of Mary Tudor three protestant martyrs suffered death by burning here. A Sessions House once stood in the street on the left where, until 1799, winter and occasional summer assizes were held. It was demolished in 1829 along with the stocks and whipping post. (N. Stephanakis collection)

→

22. 19th July 1905. We do not know what manoeuvres brought the army (or were they Volunteers?) to the High Street on this summer morning, but we do admire their choice of military transport. (W. Harding)

21. The air of a quiet country town lingers on in this view taken in 1923. Most of the buildings seen here still stand, but the wanton destruction of the chemist's shop in 1968 (it was no longer Martin's) made thinking people aware of the danger to their heritage. The public outcry led to the formation of the East Grinstead Society as a watchdog against further depredations. (F. Frith & Co.)

23. We have been unable to establish a date for this open-air service but the female costume and the almost total absence of young men in the crowd indicate the war period of 1914-18. It is perhaps a thanksgiving for the coming of peace. (N. Stephanakis collection)

EAST GRINSTEAD

SANITARY LAUNDRY

TRADE WORK

CAN NOW BE UNDERTAKEN IN LARGE OR SMALL QUANTITIES.

For Particulars and Prices apply to

THE MANAGERESS,
THE LAUNDRY,
WOOD STREET, EAST GRINSTEAD.

24. War came very close on July 9th 1943, but the damage in the High Street was insignificant compared with the tragedy that took place at the same time in the Whitehall Cinema in London Road, described later. (N. Stephanakis collection)

25. In 1890 the Round Houses were in their final stages. The four back-to-back houses were built during the late 18th century on a site that had been the town forge for some 300 years. They were up for sale when this picture was taken and were demolished during the following year. A tiny pointing hand indicates that C D Woolgar did not carry on his trade in the cellars beneath as might be supposed. The iron works were at the top of West Street. (W. Harding)

ESTABLISHED 1875. ESTABLISHED 1875.

T. & G. SMITH,

[illegible], *HIGH STREET, EAST GRINSTEAD,*

BUILDERS, SANITARY PLUMBERS

AND

HOUSE DECORATORS.

GOOD SELECTION OF CHEAP WALL-PAPERS.

E. BATSTONE

CIRCULATING LIBRARY

in connection with Mudie's.

Stationery and Fancy Goods.

SILKS, WOOLS
AND ART NEEDLEWORK

Newest Designs and Colourings

---

10 RAILWAY APPROACH

EAST GRINSTEAD

26. The Constitutional Buildings c.1905. The Round Houses were replaced by this stone building in 1893, erected for the Constitutional Club. The balcony, from which election results were announced, like the Club, is no more. In the background Clarendon House can be seen with its timbers still covered by plaster. On the right is King's cycle shop which had probably provided the penny farthing bicycle. (Town Museum collection)

Clarendon House

←

27. & 28. Judges Terrace 1907 and today. The Old Stone House (centre) is traditionally said to be the place where the judges lodged while they were conducting the Assizes. It dates from about 1590 but the extension on the right is c.1900. The adjoining Clarendon House is older; built about 1485 as a hall house, it received its present shape in Elizabethan times. Behind, the *Ship Inn* is little changed, but the timber Zion Cottage alongside has gone to make room for road improvement. Other changes are small but significant, ivy is no longer regarded as the proper adornment of an ancient building and timbering is a matter for pride and not concealment. Railings were surrendered to a World War II salvage drive.
(F. Frith & Co. and R. Michell)

29. Our pictures have led us along the south side of the High Street, and we pause on the corner of London Road before returning along the north side. In this attractive but not entirely accurate drawing, made about 1840, we see on the left the corner of the Round House platform, in the centre the old *Swan Inn*, and on the right Hayward's shop, seen better in the next picture.
(Town Museum collection)

HAYWARD.
HIGH ST, ET GRINSTEAD. 1864

LLOYDS BANK
ASHDOWN TRAVEL
GRAYS
RECORDS & VIDEO FILMS

30. The Haywards occupied the corner shop for much of the 19th century. James Hayward was stationer, newsagent, printer and publisher, and after 1870 the town postmaster as well. His son, E.S. Hayward, took over the business in 1875. The three shops next door with the tile-hung upper storeys and bow windows remain today, but the other buildings have, like Haywards, been demolished to make room for banks. (W. Harding)

31. Today the banks have taken over, and the 15th century survivor between them has had its antiquity decently covered up by new shop fronts and a new roof. (R. Michell)

32. It is 1864 and Mr Harding has set up his camera a little further up the street. Bridgland's ironmongery shop moved into London Road in the following year. Its quaint neighours seem almost ripe for demolition, though they survived for another 16 years at least. (W. Harding)

33. An uncluttered High Street that is instantly recognisable. The Capital and Counties Bank was opened in 1893 and eventually absorbed into the National Westminster. The building has now been passed to the Leeds Building Society. The 18th century block next to it was doomed to be replaced by Barclays Bank, but the elegant shopfronts were still new when this photo was taken around 1903-04. (F. Frith & Co.)

34. An annual fair first received a charter in 1247; a second fair, in December, was founded in 1516. The dates were frequently changed, but the spring and winter fairs remained important events for the town, as this view taken on April 21st 1896 shows. It was also said that fairs were an occasion for "some dissipation". (E.J. Bedford)

35. In 1984 cars replaced the cows. The drinking fountain (now dry) in the foreground commemorates the Jubilee of Queen Victoria (1887). (R. Michell)

36. The *Crown* is first mentioned in 1636 as one of the two principal inns in the town. It was a fine place for a coronation banquet, a masonic meeting or the venue for the town magistrates to hold their sessions. (W. Harding)

37. The *Crown* was substantially rebuilt in the 1870s though much old timbering remains inside. (R. Michell)

38. The well-stocked window of Messrs Young & Sons extensive grocery establishment, as seen at the end of the 19th century, shows only part of their merchandise. They also sold clothes and haberdashery at nos 43 to 49.

39. This attractive timber building, now a restaurant, was the home of Thomas Palmer who came to the town in 1775 and was appointed postmaster in 1781. It remained the town post-office until 1870 when business was transferred to Hayward's. Walter Henry Dixon took over the chemist's shop from T.J. Palmer in 1878.

MIDDLE ROW

40. The wide street was a temptation to traders to leave their stalls standing in place from week to week and ultimately to convert them into permanent structures. The process began early; in 1394 there were "four shambles standing in the Lord's High Street" and in 1425 William Neyland paid rent to build a shop there; by 1564 Middle Row was fully occupied, and some of the buildings remain to this day. 1864 is the date of this picture. The building that housed Bailye, tailor and barber, was demolished in 1877 to make way for an enlarged tailors shop. The new building covered the town well and pump, which may be seen here behind its protective railings.(W. Harding)

41. The new building may be seen at the end of the row in this picture dated 1895; it became a bank in 1920. The buildings are now smarter, but in other ways not much altered, although the prices at the Bon Marché would doubtless astound us. (F. Frith & Co.)

ESTABLISHED 1887.

W. J. S. MANN,

THE EAST GRINSTEAD

Clothier, Hosier, Hatter & Juvenile Outfitter,

Local Agent for Dr. Jaeger's Ladies' and Gentlemen's Underwear.

TAILORING DEPARTMENT, SUITS FROM 25s. TO 84s.

Best Cut, Style and Workmanship Guaranteed.

Only Address—**MIDDLE ROW, EAST GRINSTEAD.**

AGENT FOR BUTCHERS' CLOTHING.

CHURCH LANE

←

42. The east end of Middle Row was built about 1600. Before W.J.S. Mann occupied this building, it belonged to the Palmer family whom we met in charge of the post-office. They also manufactured quill pens for royalty and had the odd conceit of cutting the upper windows at the end of their shop into the shape of quills. Some of their pens may be seen in the Town Museum. The tailors however abandoned the quill windows.
(N. Stephanakis collection)

43. A short road that was the main approach to the churchyard and to the vicarage. It has changed little since Harold Connold took this view in August 1949. The 18th century house and the older tile-hung cottages which in 1694 were called "the Almshouses" are now offices. The meadow behind Sackville College is remembered as the "playfield".
(H. Connold)

ST SWITHUN'S CHURCH

44. The tower of St Swithun's dominates the town but, compared with what we have already seen, the church is not an ancient building. It was designed by the Regency architect James Wyatt and Acts of Parliament were necessary in 1790 and 1813 to raise money for its completion. The pinnacles were shortened in 1930 after one of them had been blown down in a gale. (R. Michell)

45. The old church, as it was in 1784. The accident in 1930 was the last in a series of disasters. Lightning struck the steeple in 1683 destroying both it and the tower. A century later (12th November 1785) the second tower crashed upon the body of the medieval church reducing it to ruins. (After a painting by James Lambert)

CHEQUER MEAD SCHOOL

46. The school was opened in 1861 as a National (Church) School. Boys were taught on the left and girls on the right, separated by the schoolmaster's house between. The school was extended during the 1870s and 1880s as the town population grew and by 1911, the date of this view, an infants' building on the left and a new girls' block (now the Wallis Centre) had been added behind. (F. Frith & Co.)

47. Chequer Mead Primary School today. The senior pupils moved into the new Sackville school in 1964. The name Chequer Mead was adopted from a nearby meadow as being rather more pleasant than the name of the land on which the original school stood – Slaughterhouse Mead! (R. Michell)

THE VICARAGE

48. All the land now occupied by St Swithun's Close and the car park was once part of the glebe land of the church and subsequently the garden of the vicarage. A disastrous fire on 27th February 1908 destroyed the vicarage, owing in part to a failure of the water supply. One result was the erection of the water tower that now stands on the playfield. (East Grinstead Town Museum)

→

49. & 50. In 1769 the mansion and the estate (much larger than the present grounds) was the property of John Cranston. Today, thanks to Mr Alfred Wagg who presented it to the town as a permanent War Memorial, it is the headquarters of the Town Council, a valuable social centre and the home of many activities, as well as being the location of the Town Museum. (David Kirk collection and R. Michell)

The tour of the ancient buildings of the town is now complete. The High Street and its adjacent roads, a unique survival from the past, is rightly designated as conservation area. For the rest of the town the keynote will be change and growth.

EAST COURT

LONDON ROAD

51. In the 1860s London Road, though a continuation of the turnpike, was little more than a country lane running in a north-westerly direction from the west end of the High Street. This view, looking down from the top of the town, shows on the left a saddler's shop and, slightly right of centre, the old Parish Workhouse (closed in 1861). Nothing survives today except the general configuration of the road. (W. Harding)

52. During the 1880s this part of London Road was built up, and there were new shops all the way down the eastern side. The western side was less altered, and Brinkhurst the saddlers, seen on the left, remained until the 1920s. Next to this is Armstrong, wine and spirit merchants, advertising "Allsopp's Ale & Stout". On the right is the shoe shop of Albion Russell & Son, much enlarged; it is still there, as is Armstrong's shop. (W. Harding)

53. The same scene in August 1984: 1930s shops have replaced the saddlers, but the wine merchants at no. 12 are still in their original building. A large wooden boot hangs from the shoeshop on the right, now Russell & Bromley. In the distance is the Placelands water tower, a reinforced-concrete structure erected in 1913 by A.H. Hastie because of his strong opposition to the East Grinstead Gas & Water Company. (D. Gould)

GAMLEYS

54. The London Rifle Brigade marching up London Road on 10 September 1914. The photographer, a conscientious objector, might have been expected to disapprove of this sort of thing, but nevertheless he published several patriotic postcards locally. (V.E. Morris)

→

56. This view (c.1911), taken a short distance down London Road, shows on the right Read's furniture stores; next to that, the *Warwick Arms* public house, which was destroyed by a flying bomb in July 1944; and Rice Bros.' tall building of the 1890s, also demolished by a bomb in July 1943. On the left, next to Ambridge's stores, is A.C. Taplin, stationer and newsagent, whose fine hanging enamel-plate sign reads: "For the latest news, choice cigars and tobacco, stop here." (N. Stephanakis collection)

55. A magnificent carriage and pair posed outside the *Swan Hotel,* which was owned by the Southdown & East Grinstead Breweries, later Tamplins. The landlord's name, Joseph Blakeman, is prominently displayed on the wall. Next door to the inn, Brinkhurst the saddlers is seen again. *The Swan* was closed in February 1963 and demolished.
(N. Stephanakis collection)

57. The handsome Wesleyan Chapel (S.W. Haughton, Southborough) was opened on 16 March 1881; its last service was held on 31 October 1937 and it was superseded in August 1938 by the newly built Trinity Methodist Church, in Lingfield Road. The chapel was demolished in the mid-1950s, and its site is now occupied by W.H. Smiths at no. 19. The road to the left is known as Rice's Hill since it ran through property owned by Rice Bros., agricultural engineers; the items of furniture on display were from Read's establishment, which was on the left-hand side of the hill. (W. Harding)

58. Sainsbury's premises at no. 39 having been bombed on 12 July 1944, temporary accommodation was found inside the former Wesleyan Chapel until their new superstore was opened in September 1951 at no. 37. Hygienic marble slabs on the counters are well in evidence. (N. Stephanakis collection)

59. Mrs George Read carried on the furniture business at 19/21 London Road long after the death of her husband. Mr Ward (manager) and Mr Funnell (assistant) are standing outside. The building was bombed in July 1944. (N. Stephanakis collection)

60. Read's furniture delivery van, built by Thornycroft, was in use from March 1923 to November 1929. In common with many vehicles of this period, it ran on solid tyres. (Thornycroft/East Grinstead Town Museum)

→

62. The Whitehall, October 1984. Its architect was F. Edward Jones, and it was opened on 16 November 1936; it contained a cinema, ballroom and restaurant. The shops on the right date from 1951. (D. Gould)

61. In this c.1905 view we see F. Cruttenden & Co., jewellers, and in the same block Rice Bros., saddlers, cycle factors and implement agents. Next door, at nos. 33/35, Bridglands, ironmongers, whose building received a direct hit from the air on 9 July 1943. In the distance, where the road curves, may be seen the handsome Literary and Scientific Institute building, opened November 1888. (East Grinstead Photo Co.)

63. Looking south-east up London Road in 1907, with a closer view of Bridglands, who among their multifarious activities sold "motor spirit" over the counter. All the buildings in the foreground were destroyed in 1943 and 1944. In 1951 entirely new shops were opened on this side in neo-Georgian style, extending from nos. 23 to 43. (F. Frith & Co.)

THE

EAST GRINSTEAD CARRIAGE FACTORY,

LONDON ROAD, EAST GRINSTEAD.

ALFRED RICE,

MANUFACTURER OF

EVERY DESCRIPTION of CARRIAGES.

ANY KIND OF MOTOR CAR BUILT TO ORDER.

Repairs and Upholstering Carefully Executed.

CARRIAGES AND LIGHT CARTS OF ALL KINDS BUILT TO ORDER.

REPAIRS OF EVERY DESCRIPTION Promptly Executed by Experienced Workmen.

64. The North Sussex Garage, at 36 London Road, was opened by Rice Bros. in 1912. It was adjacent to King's Garage, run by W. & H. King, and they were deadly rivals. This 1920s interior scene shows, in the foreground, a Singer 10-hp 2-seater, which was driven by Joe Rice junior. The car next to it is an Albert; also visible are a Ford Model T and Unic hire-car. (N. Stephanakis collection)

65. Frontage of the North Sussex Garage, on which its building date is proclaimed as 1912. The garage was severely damaged in the last war, and a new shop was built on its site in 1950, originally a drapers, and now a shoe shop. (N. Stephanakis collection)

66. This ancient smithy at no. 48, London Road, was run by Mr Burgess in its last years and was replaced, in the early 1920s, by a row of shops at nos. 48, 50 and 52. (N. Stephanakis collection)

P. E. TOMBS,

Newsagent, Stationer and Tobacconist,

18, LONDON ROAD.

ALL DAILY AND WEEKLY PAPERS PROMPTLY DELIVERED.

Picture Postcards of the District

ALWAYS IN STOCK.

68. Interior of the Whitehall Theatre and Ballroom which was tragically destroyed. On 9 July 1943 a lone raider dropped a stick of bombs across the town killing 108 people, a figure which included many children. Most of those who died were attending a matinee performance in this Cinema, which received a direct hit. (H. Connold)

67. The Grosvenor Hall (1883) was adapted in 1910 as the Whitehall Cinema – East Grinstead's first – and Restaurant by its owners, the caterers Letheby & Christopher. This was rebuilt into the present Whitehall and reopened on 16 November 1936. The block adjacent to the Whitehall – nos. 37 to 45 – was destroyed by a flying bomb on 12 July 1944. On the right in this 1921 view is the row of shops that replaced the smithy, and, further up, the rival King's and North Sussex motor garages. (F. Frith & Co.)

69. The parade down London Road for the coronation of King George V in 1911. This view from Rock Gardens was a favourite one for photographers recording street processions. (A. Harding)

70. It was the custom for Election results to be declared from Rock Gardens (nos. 49, 51 and 53, London Road; now Whitehall Parade). Here is the declaration of the poll on 28 January 1910, when Henry Cautley (Conservative) defeated the Liberal, C.H. Corbett. Mr Cautley was to remain East Grinstead's M.P. until 1936, when he received a peerage. (A. Harding)

71. The bombing of London Road in the late afternoon of 9 July 1943 resulted in the destruction of Bridglands and Rice Bros. buildings, as well as the Whitehall Cinema. The frontage of the latter was little damaged.

72. Milepost 30, photographed in 1985, outside the former offices of the *East Grinstead Observer,* seen in picture no. 75. This late 18th-century cast-iron post is one of the "Bow Bells" series, erected along the Eastbourne and Lewes roads by the turnpike trusts, who were required by law to erect milestones. East Grinstead is exactly 30 miles from London both by road and by rail.
(R. Michell)

73. A postcard of about 1909 of London Road by the post office, which was opened by the Duke of Norfolk on 16 September 1896. Queens Road comes in on the left; it was named Cemetery Road until 1887. The pace of life in this scene seems very leisured; three groups of people are enjoying conversations.
(P.E. Tombs/East Grinstead Town Museum)

74. The same location, as seen in August 1984. On the right is King Street, laid out about 1934. The splendid avenue of elms seen in the previous photograph gave way to shops in the 1920s and 1930s. (D. Gould)

75. Looking up London Road from King Street in 1937, after the new Whitehall frontage had been built but before the demolition of the Literary & Scientific Institute on the corner. On the right is the *East Grinstead Observer* office, built in 1891 by Edward Steer for *his* newspaper, the short-lived *Southern Free Press,* which was bought by the *Observer,* who then occupied the building until November 1981. The little block of shops between the *Observer* and the post office comprised: 70 – Fry, butcher; 72 – Francis, confectioner; 74 – Coughtrey, hairdresser and 76 – Kale, tobacconist. (F. Frith & Co.)

→

76. The canyon-like appearance of London Road, curving as it rises, is well brought-out in this October 1984 view. McIlroy's store, built in 1938, has replaced the Institute, and beyond the Whitehall are the post-war neo-Georgian buildings that filled in the large gap left by bombing. The right-hand pavement was widened in 1983 to make the road the same width all the way down. It is most unusual to see a policeman on point duty at the crossroads; the traffic signals had failed. (D. Gould)

WILSON'S

C.M. WILSON LTD

78-86 London Road · 1·3·5 & 7 Queens Road

'Phone 25 East Grinstead

Household Linens.

Drapery . .

Millinery .

Underwear

Hosiery . . .

We do not keep

EVERYTHING

BUT—

We have in stock the fashion goods in Ladies' wear and Gentlemen's wear that are popular at the moment in addition to those goods of every-day use, and honest value is the foundation upon which we are building our business.

Gentlemen's Outfitting

Tailoring

House . . Furniture

Value Will Tell.

77. In this 1909 view a splendid tree may be seen where King Street later came in. The shops in the foreground all survive though in different ownerships: no. 71, Home & Colonial Tea Stores; 65, Humphrey, fishmonger and 63, Williams, stationer. No. 61 was added in the 1930s. On the right is C.M. Wilson, draper, whose shop had the longest frontage in London Road and who was in business from 1887 to June 1965.
(F. Frith & Co.)

78. A cycle event near the junction of Railway Approach. The dwarf was "Biggie" Raw. The shops, built about 1905, are: 104, Curtis the baker; 106, W. Hitch; 108, London Central Meat Co. (purpose-built as a fire station and replaced by 1906 – the lookout turret is visible); and 110/112, Dixon the chemists, who also had a branch in the High Street. In the background is the *Railway Hotel* of 1856. (N. Stephanakis collection)

Telephone No. 9.

RICE BROS., LIMITED,

ENGINEERS, IMPLEMENT AGENTS AND SADDLERS,

CYCLE FACTORS and SPORTS OUTFITTERS.

REPAIRS to all kinds of ENGINES and MACHINERY by Competent Workmen.

WE ARE AGENTS FOR ALL THE BEST MAKES OF

CYCLES.

TRAVELLING TRUNKS, SUIT CASES AND LEATHER BAGS.

Large Stock of Reliable Goods at Lowest Prices.

Come and inspect our "SEVEN STAR" SEWING MACHINE, with Walnut Cover, &c., complete, at £2. 15s.

Office and Works: 29, LONDON ROAD, EAST GRINSTEAD.

Branch Depôts at Edenbridge, Haywards Heath, Blindley Heath and elsewhere.

79. The *Railway Hotel* in 1923. This was owned by brewers Nalder & Collyer, and was also accommodation for the Cyclists' Touring Club. (F. Frith & Co.)

81. In this August 1984 view, almost all the buildings seen in the previous picture are still there, but the road layout has altered. The *Glanfield* is set further back than its predecessor. (D. Gould)

80. The same scene in 1937. The *Railway Hotel* is still there, but was demolished and replaced by the *Glanfield* (named after its architect) in 1939. The fine avenue of elms went in 1925 to make way for Fosters Garage and shops. The bus, on route 409 from Forest Row to West Croydon, is an ex-London General Regent of 1931. It appears that the conductor has failed to alter his destination blind! (F. Frith & Co.)

82. 140 London Road was the Urban District Council's fire brigade station from about 1906 to 1923. It was manned by part-time, voluntary firemen. Standing outside, from left to right, are: E. Perrins, Tom Simmons, Captain William Simmons and George Simmons. The Simmons family served on the brigade for a great many years; George was 75 when he resigned, the town's oldest fireman. (N. Stephanakis collection)

83. The original White Lion Inn in the 1860s. (W. Harding)

84. The present White Lion, opened in December 1965, is the third to occupy this site. For its period it is a remarkably handsome building. (D. Gould)

85. London Road looking north-west at the junction of Moat Road, which was laid out about 1871 by the builder, Edward Steer. The shop on the corner was demolished in 1982. (East Grinstead Photo Co.)

86. In this view of September 1984 we see modern frontages at nos. 182 and 184, which replaced cottages; then the older block (186 to 192) seen in the previous picture; the Roman Catholic church (opened on 2 October 1898); and a further row of shops beyond. (D. Gould)

87. This row of shops at nos. 186-192 London Road still stands, dominated by the massive Roman Catholic church. Before the Great War their owners were: W.J. Wood & Co., general stores, displaying outside zinc baths, pails, wicker clothes-baskets and spades; Brockhurst Dairy; D. Streeter, antiques (he had moved across the road to no. 193 by 1916) and E. Beard, confectioner.
(N. Stephanakis collection)

CANTELUPE ROAD

88. East Grinstead Motor Coaches, owned by H.J. Sargent, ran stage-carriage services and private-hire coaches from the 1920s until 1951, when the business was sold to Southdown Motor Services. The three coaches seen outside the Cantelupe Road garage in the 1930s include a Star and two Gilfords. (H. Connold)

CANTELUPE LAUNDRY,

CANTELUPE ROAD.

Manageress:—MISS BURGEN.

This Laundry is under the supervision of Ladies, and it is absolutely guaranteed that **No Chemicals are used.**

ALL HAND WORK. **INSPECTION INVITED.**

Price List on application to the Manageress.

90. A similar view in August, 1984. The surviving house, Hill Cottage (seen in the centre of the previous view), has had structural alterations, and a hedge has replaced the iron railings. (D. Gould)

COLLEGE LANE

89. College Lane, named after Sackville College, runs north from the east end of the High Street to Blackwell Hollow. This view, looking north, shows a weatherboarded cottage and a group of children in 1907. This building no longer exists; there is just a rough, grassed bank marking its site. (F. Frith & Co.)

91. The northern end of College Lane where it leads into Blackwell Hollow, with the entrance to East Court on the right. East Court had been built for John Cranston in 1769. The land bordering the lower part of Blackwell Hollow was conveyed to the town in 1894 by Dr C.H. Gatty and no building was permitted there. (N. Stephanakis collection)

92. At the top of Blackwell Hollow in August 1984, with a bus for Horsham emerging into College Lane. The stone wall is still there but the entrance to East Court is much changed, and now Estcots Drive (1974) comes in on the right. (D. Gould)

SHIP STREET

93. The scene is almost unrecognisable, yet nearly all the buildings are still there: the 18th-century artisans' cottages and the Ship Inn, seen in the background. This name has been traced back to the late 17th century and is presumed by some to be a corruption of the word "sheep"; it is also thought that the street was named after the inn. (W. Page)

94. The foliage is less, the traffic is more, but externally at least, the cottages are unchanged. This view is from the opposite direction to the previous one. (R. Michell)

Grinstead, The Dove Cote

95. Ship Street leads out of the town to Dunnings. On the way there, one may observe this magnificent Gatehouse, built about 1862. To the left of the driveway there is a round turret, the Dovecote; unfortunately it is not possible to include both parts of the building in one photograph. This view dates from 1907. (F. Frith & Co.)

WEST STREET

97. Zion Chapel, opened in 1811, had nothing to do with Zionists. It was used by Calvinistic Methodists under the patronage of the Countess of Huntingdon. The building is considered to be one of the finest in the town dating from the early nineteenth century. Now known as West Street Evangelical Church, it is used by Baptists formerly at Providence Chapel, London Road, and is a Grade II listed building. (R. Michell)

96. This is the present appearance of the Dovecote and Gatehouse, which has been modified by making one house into two and by converting the through drive into an extra room. (D. Gould)

WEST HILL

98. Old Mill Lane was by 1911 also known as West Hill. A watermill had once existed at the bottom of the hill. The wall on the left of this picture of about 1902 is still there, but little else is recognisable today. The entrance to Queens Road Cemetery (opened in 1869) is on the right.
(W. Tomlinson/N. Stephanakis collection)

99. Looking down West Hill from the same spot, August 1984. Queens Road cemetery now has no entrance from Queens Road; the West Hill entrance here shown is the only access point. (D. Gould)

QUEENS ROAD

100. Originally called Cemetery Road (because it led to the cemetery) it was renamed Queens Road in 1887, Queen Victoria's jubilee year; at first the name change was unofficial – the residents disliked the official name – and later the road was extended past the cemetery to West Street. This building was opened on 22 December 1879 as a coffee tavern, but it was unsuccessful. It was leased to the Ragged School Union on 2 September 1885, in whose use it is here shown as "Holiday Home No. 2". The building was converted and extended as a cottage hospital and was opened on 15 October 1902, remaining as such until 1936, when the Literary and Scientific Institute took it over.
(N. Stephanakis collection)

101. The building, here shown virtually as converted in 1902 (although this is the front; in the previous view we saw the side and back), was empty in 1984, having been used as offices for some time. Until the last war there were iron railings fronting the left-hand bay; those on the right have survived the "war effort" because they prevent passers-by from falling into the basement.
(D. Gould)

KING STREET

102. This street, opposite the Queens Road entry into London Road, was laid out about 1934 as part of a development of this area by William Christopher, of the catering firm Letheby & Christopher. The magnificent Radio Centre cinema, which accommodated 1200 people, was named after Radio City Theatre in New York. Designed by F. Edward Jones, it was opened on 11 April 1936, the first film shown being Jack Hulbert's "Jack of all trades". Caffyns motor garage, from the same period, is also rather splendid. The film being shown is "Dishonour Bright" starring Tom Walls, a popular comedian in the 1930s.

103. East Grinstead is fortunate indeed in still having a functioning cinema, as seen in this 1984 view. The Radio Centre was renamed the Classic in 1966, and in August 1972 it was converted into two cinemas plus a bingo hall. A third cinema was added in January 1973. Caffyns meanwhile has lost most of its cream tiles, but is still very handsome. (D. Gould)

CINEMA DE LUXE

EAST GRINSTEAD.

MANAGER - ARTHUR IZON　　　Phone **277** East Grinstead.

6.0　CONTINUOUS PERFORMANCE　10.15

MATINEES, TUESDAY, THURSDAY AND SATURDAY at **3**

The Small House

With a Big Reputation

Always a Bright and Up-to-date Programme of Quality

Popular Prices 1/6 1/2 1/- 6*d.* & 4*d.*

RAILWAY APPROACH

104. Laid out in the 1860s, Glen Vue Road originally led to the Workhouse. Twenty years later is became built up and several shops were opened on the south side. It was renamed Railway Approach in September 1906. In this view looking east, taken on a fine summer's evening in the early part of this century, the four shops nearest the camera are, from left to right: Streatfield, grocer; Major, jeweller (both had moved to London Road by 1916); the East Grinstead Photo Co. (run by E. Kinsey – still there in 1928) and Mugridge, butcher.
(East Grinstead Photo Co.)

→

106. At the bottom of Railway Approach stood the grim Union Workhouse, opened in 1860 and known as The Spike. Tramps were lined up each evening for admission. In recent years it became St Leonards Hospital, and was demolished in March 1982, though part of it on the other side of the road survives in the Mid Sussex Timber Co. premises.
(W. Harding)

105. A modern view shows that the buildings are still all there, but each has been altered in some way: new shop fronts, brickwork painted or rendered, slates replaced by tiles. However, Railway Approach remains one of the most characterful shopping streets in the town, provided as it is with numerous small individual shops. (D. Gould)

MOAT ROAD

107. Foster steam tractor of the "Wellington" type, owned by William Best and Son, coal merchants of East Grinstead, stands in Moat Road outside the photographer's premises in about 1910. The locomotive was registered in Lincoln about 1908. The man in the centre is Ernest Creasey. Faintly discernible in the background is the water tower, now gone, of the East Grinstead Gas & Water Co. (William Page)

→

109. The old malthouse is now the headquarters of the Royal British Legion and ex-servicemen and women's club. The maltster's cottage has been demolished, and the big sweep coming into the foreground is part of the one-way road system from Station Road to London Road. (N. Stephanakis)

STATION ROAD

108. Station Road was laid out about 1882, at the time the new two-level station was being built. Near its junction with London Road stood the malthouse of the Southdown and East Grinstead Breweries; the maltster lived in the cottage on the left. On the wall of the malthouse is a board advertising William Best's furniture depository; not only was he a coal and corn merchant, but he undertook "household removals by road or rail". The small boy in the picture is his son Albert. (W. Page)

110. At the corner of Station Road and London Road, William Best had built, in 1887, a shop and house, living there until about 1908. The boy on the pony is Albert Best. Holmden's, the corn merchants in the large adjacent building, bought the shop in about 1942 and Best & Son moved to 176a London Road, from where the coal delivery business flourished until October 1975. The whole block on the corner was demolished to make way for the road realignment in connection with the one-way system.
(A. Harding)

112. Station Road in August 1984. Undesirable changes include machine-made pantiles which have replaced the slates; monstrous lamp-posts; and a road surface plastered with lettering. All the cast-iron gates and fencing that once protected the gardens disappeared in the last war. At least the ivy has been stripped from the centre house, no. 19, as one improvement.
(D. Gould)

111. Station Road in 1907. All the houses still exist; no. 18, the three-storey building in the centre, was occupied by the Citizen's Advice Bureau from 1975 until 1983. The railway to London runs parallel in a deep cutting on the left. The road is now a one-way racetrack and it would be unwise and illegal to ride one's bicycle in the direction shown here. (F. Frith & Co.)

113. Nutt Brothers ran livery stables and horse cabs from premises at the bottom of Station Road. In 1914 the first motor car was purchased and car-hire was added to the services provided. In this picture is a smart 1921 Unic, painted a shade of green known as "Dutch pink", which gave it a brown tinge! It was a show-model at the 1921 Motor Show. The proprietor was Harold Hewitt Nutt, the photographer's father. (K. Nutt)

NUTT BROS.

HUNTING & LIVERY STABLES, :: :: ::

STATION ROAD,

EAST GRINSTEAD.

HUNTERS, HACK AND HARNESS HORSES of every description on :: Sale or Hire.

LESSONS IN RIDING AND DRIVING.

GOOD LOOSE BOXES FOR HORSES STANDING AT LIVERY.

114. This photograph shows Nutt Bros. petrol pump, a 1926 Morris Cowley, and the High Level platforms of the railway station. The owner of the car is W. Lambert, who for many years was manager of the local Hall & Co. yard. At the pump is H. Nutt's employee Bert Buddle; he is wearing a bow tie, for he was also a chauffeur for the firm. (K. Nutt)

115. Kenneth Nutt took over the business in 1948 on the death of his father, running it as "Nutt's Garage" until 1966 when he sold out to the Cleveland Petrol Co. It is now Brooklands Service Station. The central building is all that survives of the collection of stables, sheds and outbuildings that once comprised the Nutt Bros. enterprise. (D. Gould)

ESTABLISHED 40 YEARS.

Telephone :
EAST GRINSTEAD 12.

Telegrams :
NUTT, EAST GRINSTEAD 12.

NUTT BROS.

CARS FOR HIRE

CARS GARAGED. PETROLS, OILS, ETC.

:: Hunting Stables and Riding Lessons ::

Station Road, East Grinstead

ONE MINUTE from RAILWAY STATION.

ST. MARGARET'S CONVENT

116. An early view of this Anglican convent, taken from the driveway which ran from Moat Road. It was the home of the Sisterhood of St Margaret, founded in 1855 by the Rev J.M. Neale. The first stone was laid on 20 July 1865, and the convent was ready for occupation in 1870. The magnificent Chapel, prominent in this view, was designed by G.E. Street and opened on 24 February 1883. Recently the Sisters moved to a new convent and the old one was converted into private flats, the chapel falling out of use.
(N. Stephanakis collection)

THE RAILWAY

117. Engineers' ballast train stands in the cutting north of East Grinstead station about 1882, before the opening of the Oxted line in March 1884. The locomotive is *Cliftonville;* it had been used on the Cliftonville Spur contract, building the Preston Park – Hove link line from 1876 to 1879. Top right is the farmland which was sold for building Grosvenor and Crescent Roads in about 1905. The station is in the distance. The railways that once served the town are fully described and illustrated in *Branch Lines to East Grinstead* (Middleton Press). (W. Page)

118. East Grinstead station building, photographed in about 1905. Also seen are most of the station staff and the Company's delivery cart, no. 248. The building, designed by T.H. Myres of Preston, was in existence from 1882 to 1971, after which a prefabricated structure replaced it. (A. Harding)

119. A London Brighton & South Coast Railway scene, but taken on 1 September 1923, the first year of the Southern Railway's 25-year life. A tank locomotive takes water at the station's only water crane, at the west end of the high-level station. Grosvenor Road is seen ending at the Company's boundary fence. There is now a large car park where these trains once ran. (K. Nutt)

120. Photographed in 1960, this view from the high level station (then still open) of the railway leading northwards from the low level station may still be seen, but from a public footbridge built on the site of these platforms. The high level station was closed on 1st January 1967 and subsequently demolished. The telegraph poles, so typical of a traditional railway, have also vanished. With this scene of the children awaiting a train, we take our leave of East Grinstead Then and Now. (Norman Sherry)